MAKING MORAL
DECISIONS

MAKING MORAL DECISIONS

J. Philip Wogaman

ABINGDON PRESS
Nashville

MAKING MORAL DECISIONS

Copyright © 1990 by Abingdon Press

This book is printed on acid-free paper.

Library of Congress Cataloging-in-Publication Data

WOGAMAN, J. PHILIP.
    Making moral decisions / J. Philip Wogaman.
        p.   cm. — (Faithful congregations series)
    Includes bibliographical references.
    ISBN 0-687-12654-1 (pbk. : alk paper)
    1. Christian ethics—Methodist authors. 2. Church renewal—United States. 3. Pastoral theology—Methodist Church 4. Methodist Church—Doctrines. 5. United Methodist Church (U.S.)—Doctrines. 6. Liberalism (Religion)—Protestant churches. I. Title. II. Series.
BJ1251.W5826   1990
241—dc20   90-21920
                                                                    CIP

Scripture quotations unless otherwise noted are from the New Revised Standard Version of the Bible, copyright 1989 by the Division of Christian Education of the National Council of Churches of Christ in the USA.

MANUFACTURED IN THE UNITED STATES OF AMERICA

Contents

Preface

But speaking the truth in love, we must grow up in every way into him who is the head, into Christ. (EPHESIANS 4:15)

It is not always easy for Christians to "speak the truth in love" to one another within the fellowship of the church. Sometimes, obsessed by our own version of the truth, we thrust it upon others unlovingly. Sometimes, fearful of division within the church, we avoid expressing opinions on all controversial subjects. We have a hard time putting truth and love together. But that is what this book is about. It is written to help local churches learn how to explore moral issues, even controversial ones, together.

I am convinced that honest dialogue, in a spirit of love, is a very important part of being a faithful congregation. It is not a very loving thing to avoid the truth about things that matter. And, in the Christian sense of the word, it is not very truthful to express our views unlovingly. We have much to learn from one another about the personal and social problems and issues that concern us most. The church is exactly the right place for those matters to be discussed. Far from disrupting the church, honest and loving dialogue helps build it up, while also giving each of us greater insight into the problems we face in this perplexing world.

In writing this book, I have myself learned much from the honest (and loving) criticism of the following people who read the entire manuscript: Kenneth L. Carder, Alan Geyer, John D. Godsey, Jack Keller, Donna Linksz, James Nash, Betty Willson, Janet Wolf, and Carroll Yingling. Besides my Abingdon Press editor, this group includes lay people, local church pastors, and seminary colleagues. They have inflicted real improvements upon the book, but they are not to be held accountable for the remaining imperfections. A similar word of thanks goes to my wife Carolyn, whose quiet encouragement and good sense have been as indispensable in this as in my previous writing.

My clergy and lay colleagues of the Baltimore Annual Conference of the United Methodist Church have taught me much about how the church can engage in dialogue on difficult questions without breaking the bonds of love and peace. I wish to dedicate this small book to them in the hope that it will be a help to them and others like them who serve the church.

J. Philip Wogaman

Wesley Theological Seminary

Washington, D.C.

1

An Uncertain Church in a Troubled World

Nobody doubts that this is a troubled world. We can rejoice that the shadow of nuclear war has lifted somewhat in the easing of Cold War tensions. We can celebrate the movement toward democracy in dozens of countries. And we can applaud the technical developments with computers and communications. But we have become all the more aware of the poverty haunting half the population of the world, violence stalking the streets of great cities, and threats to the global environment and peace. We are torn apart by conflict over abortion, homosexuality, and drugs. We are perplexed by the implications of biotechnology. And we are outraged by revelations of corruption in business and politics.

That is exactly the world the church finds itself in. How does a faithful congregation address such a world?

An acquaintance of mine, who is pastor of an inner-city church, was robbed at gunpoint and beaten a few months ago. The people of the congregation expressed sympathetic concern. Some of the men voiced surprise, however, upon learning that the pastor did not carry a gun himself. Over half of the men of the congregation were armed, they said, even when attending church. This horrified my friend even more than being mugged. But it also deepened his perplexity about how a congregation can exert moral leadership in the midst of a troubled city.

Another local congregation faces the problem of ministry to persons of homosexual orientation. Recently this local church struggled with the question of whether it should recognize and facilitate "holy unions" for same-sex couples. Would this be understood as a caring ministry for people who have no choice over their sexual orientation, thus helping them achieve stable, long-term relationships? Or would it be understood as freezing them in an unhealthy, unchristian pattern of behavior? How could such an issue be resolved?

Members of yet another local church, located in the farm belt, are watching their community erode before their very eyes as one family farm after another goes into bankruptcy. How are they to understand and deal with these economic forces?

Still another local congregation includes a number of nuclear physicists. They have been troubled by the potential use of their work in contributing to nuclear holocaust or environmental hazards. But they have not felt understood or supported much by their fellow Christians.

The vocational quandaries of these scientists are repeated in countless ways by Christian doctors, lawyers, teachers, civil servants, union members, farmers, businesspersons, homemakers, salespersons, and unskilled laborers, who confront moral dilemmas in their daily work. Does the church expect them to divorce their work from their identity as Christians? Can their fellow Christians in the church help them think this through?

When we think of faithful congregations we tend to think of their spirit and their activities more than their thinking. Such a local congregation is one that seems spiritually alive and busily engaged in doing good works. It is a caring church in which people of all kinds feel at home. It has strong evangelistic outreach, with statistically measurable results.

We tend not to think of a vital church as a community of moral discourse, where Christians struggle together to understand the implications of their faith in a troubled world. It is easier to speak of love in the church than it is to speak of discernment. It is easier for the church to act than to know why and for what ultimate purpose it is acting. But can the church put the loving and the acting and the thinking together? That is the question to which this book is directed.

Moral Issues and Problems

We tend to understand moral questions too narrowly. We may think of morality as having to do only with sexual behavior and honesty in our business dealings—and morality surely has to do with such things. But morality is a much bigger subject. It includes everything we do to live our lives and organize our world in accordance with our deepest values. For Christians, those values are drawn from the heart of their faith as Christians. Those values represent what seems, in light of that faith, to be good. Evil, on the other hand, is what obstructs the good. So, for Christians, morality is living one's whole life as a Christian; it is acting in the world so as to exert a Christian influence in behalf of good and in opposition to evil.

A moral "problem" for Christians, therefore, is a point

11

where Christian values are threatened. What is understood by some people to be a "problem" may not be perceived as a problem by others. Racism, for instance, was not considered to be a problem by Americans and South Africans who believed in segregation or apartheid, but it surely was a problem for the victims. Low wages may not be perceived as a problem by businesspersons who are eager to cut operating costs; almost certainly low wages will be seen as a problem by workers trying to make ends meet. The drug problem is not a problem to those engaged in the drug traffic; it definitely is a problem to people who care about the devastation of lives and communities accompanying the sale and use of drugs. We always define problems on the basis of what we care about. So, for Christians, moral problems are defined theologically—that is, by reference to what we believe in and worship. For Christians, moral problems are based on how God views the world: Where are the obstructions to God's loving purposes? Where are the opportunities for healing the brokenness of the world and for fulfilling the possibilities God has created? What are the special opportunities and dangers in the lives of individual persons?

But moral problems do not necessarily become issues for debate. Moral "issues" represent disagreements over how to define and deal with problems. Often, they have to do with decisions and policies. A real issue is one where there is genuine disagreement and where some kind of case can be made by all those engaged in the debate.

The Changing Stream of Issues

Methodist churches of the 1830s and 1840s were caught up in the slavery controversy, an issue that was to break apart both the church and the nation. Following the Civil War, slavery as such was no longer an issue, but the status of former slaves was—and this was soon to be joined by the issues of woman suffrage and the prohibition of beverage alcohol. Issues related to the labor movement occupied the church from around 1910 to after World War II. Debate over issues of equality has gripped the church through much of the twentieth century, with particular attention being given to the civil rights movement and equal rights for women.

Some issues are resolved one way or another; some just seem to go away. The issue of slavery was resolved, as was that of woman suffrage. The Prohibition issue, years after the Great Experiment, seems simply to have gone away—though the problems associated with the issue may be as severe now as they were at the turn of the century. Some of the civil rights issues were settled, we hope, once and for all. It is no longer debatable whether church segregation should be allowed or whether there should be separate sections of buses and trains for persons of different color. On such issues, at least among thinking people, it is clear now that one side was essentially right and the other essentially wrong. When such a conclusion has been reached within the church, an issue is no longer there to be joined—even though the problem, or remnants of the problem, may still exist to some extent.

Today, in the world of the 1990s, some old issues are still with us, and some new ones are developing. The poverty problem, hotly debated within the churches in the 1960s, remains a substantial issue in church and society. Communism, in the wake of the transformations in the USSR and Eastern Europe, may no longer be much of an issue. But issues concerning political and economic ideology continue to stimulate serious debate. With the apparent end of the Cold War, world trade relationships and the building of international institutions of all sorts may create a whole new series of issues for debate. Biotechnology, with startling new insights and developments, may not yet be well enough understood to fuel a significant debate within the churches. But one suspects that that may be just around the corner as we confront this or that vision of the brave new world, with its perils and possibilities.

To summarize: what is a *problem* to some people may not be a problem to others, depending upon the values we hold and our perceptions of reality. If one is a Christian, one's values will presumably have a very important effect upon what one considers to be a problem. Moral *issues*, on the other hand, are disagreements giving rise to debate as the church and community consider alternative ways of understanding and dealing with problems.

Individual vs. Corporate Response

Problems and issues are inescapably social, since all of us live in a social context. But this does not mean that individual Christians do not have important moral responsibility in their personal lives. Most of us live and work in a variety of settings, more or less simultaneously. We may have a home, a job, recreational activities, consumer decisions to be made, educational pursuits, and our life and work in a local church. The resolution of the big social issues confronting church and society is bound to affect most of our social roles. But in the meantime, we also have to act.

Part of the uncertainty confronting the church is how it can best help its members address their personal moral dilemmas. It may be that sweeping political and economic changes are needed. But, meantime, how should Christians think and act in the world as it is given to them? What help can be given to Christians in business, in law, in medicine, in education, in agriculture, in organized labor? How should Christians deal with changing patterns of family life, including changes in the roles of women and men and changing patterns of child-rearing?

Two things can be said about this. First, every Christian should have at the same time some conception of social reforms that are needed and some conception of how to deal responsibly in the world before the reforms have been accomplished. Second, given the realities of human sinfulness and the limits to human knowledge, the church cannot anticipate perfection within the course of human history. So, in coming to terms with this world, individual Christians need all the help they can get. The moral dialogue within the church must address both the wider problems facing the world corporately and institutionally and the more personal problems confronting faithful Christians within that world.

2

Is the Church the Place for Moral Dialogue?

Some people still question whether the church is the proper place for discussion of controversial moral issues. Four very different kinds of objections have been raised. Obviously there is no point to a book like this if the church is *not* a proper place for moral dialogue, so we must pause to consider the objections. But perhaps the objections may also help us clarify the responsibility of the church to be such a place.

Objections

Objection One: The church should be concerned about individual salvation and spiritual life, not about political and materialistic questions. Such objections have a very long history. The Social Gospel pioneers of the early twentieth century had to confront the argument that they were "unspiritual" and that the affairs of the world were better left to practical business leaders and politicians who knew something about them.

17

Controversial issues were held to be divisive in the life of the church, dividing Christian against Christian. The church should be a place of refuge from the currents and conflicts of the world, not the arena where such conflicts are fought out.

Such objections are, in fact, much older than the controversies over the Social Gospel movement. Amaziah the priest of Bethel offered such objections to the prophet Amos, questioning Amos' motives and his loyalties (Amos 7:10-17). During the Gnostic controversies of the first and second centuries A.D., a major effort was mounted by such Christian leaders as Marcion to redefine Christian faith in wholly spiritual terms. That effort was successfully resisted by those who shaped orthodox Christian doctrine in the early centuries, but such spiritualism has resurfaced periodically throughout Christian history.

What is wrong with it? Surely the church *is* concerned about individual salvation and spiritual life. The gospel of grace and salvation, with its affirmation that every single person matters to God, is at the heart of the Christian message. And that same gospel emphasizes the life of the spirit against a purely materialistic view of life. We are told, in Matthew and Luke, that "you cannot serve God and wealth" (Matt. 6:24; Luke 16:13).

But Christian theologians have also understood from the beginning that God's gift of creation is important alongside the life of the spirit. We are not created as disembodied spirits; we are born into a quite physical world with quite physical needs requiring fulfillment in quite physical ways. In this world, the life of the spirit depends upon a material context for its expression. The New Testament book of Colossians speaks of the relationship between Christ and the material universe: "for in him all things in heaven and on earth were created . . . and in him all things hold together"

(Col. 1:16*a*, 17*b*). The implication of this theological view is that the material world is a part of the plan of God; it is not an accident or a mistake. God's spiritual purposes can be frustrated when obstructed in the material realm. Thus, God's loving intentions for hungry children in a famine-stricken Third World country (or an American city) can be obstructed by malnutrition. Jesus' own ministry of healing illustrates the point that disease can also stand in the way.

The early twentieth-century theologian Walter Rauschen-busch contributed a further point, however. It is that we are inescapably caught up in social, political, and economic systems that either reinforce or undermine our moral commitments. In speaking of an unchristian social order, he points out that it makes good people do bad things—just as a Christian social order can make bad people do good things. Such language is oversimplified. But it contains the insight that ordinary, normal life in an evil society almost forces people to do evil things as a matter of course—while selfish, unjust people are less able to exploit or oppress others if institutions exist to prevent that behavior.

Human life is interconnected. We do not exist as solitary individuals. If the church is to address its members at all, it must be as persons in community who live in a physical world! And if we are to be faithful to the total gospel we must address its social implications.

Objection Two: The church's task is to be the church, to be true to its own story, thus constituting a model of what the world should be. This way of phrasing an objection is rather new, although the point itself is quite old. The point is not based on a false spiritualism or individualism. It is, rather, that there is no point in trying to relate to the world on its own terms. The world is essentially fallen. The world outside the church does not share the church's values, and there is no point in conducting a moral dialogue within the church about policies that must be adopted by those outside the church. Our task is not to clarify moral decisions to be made; it is rather to be authentically formed by the "story"—the history and traditions—that have made our community of faith what it is. Being faithful to our story within our community is the best way to bear witness to those on the outside. Perhaps they will be attracted by what they see and want to learn more about it. In some respects, this view may be a modern-day expression of the older monastic impulse, though there are important differences as well.

The problem is that we are already involved in that society outside the church, like it or not. There is no way we can avoid being implicated in its evils if we are a part of it. As Rauschenbusch understood, just by being normal participants in economic and political institutions, we contribute to their purposes—even if we abhor those purposes. Moreover, from a theological standpoint, we do well not to underestimate the extent to which God is also at work in the world beyond the church—nor to overestimate the extent to which sin has permeated the church. In truth, the whole world is God's world. The whole world is the arena for the struggle for redemption and God's intended good.

Objection Three: We already have the important answers—the important things are commitment and action, not further talk. Some years ago, when making a report on a study process about infant-formula marketing to a general church gathering, I was challenged by one of the members. "How long," she wanted to know, "are we going to continue studying these questions while the babies are dying?" Her question made sense only if one assumed, as she did, that the answers were already in.

In most of the church debates over the past decade or two,

there have been people who have similarly assumed that the answers were already in. Indeed, sometimes the important answers *are* already in! Would it not seem strange to have a serious church dialogue over the desirability of reinstituting slavery or abolishing the general right of citizens to vote or whether women should be allowed to speak in church? At one time, these were serious issues to be debated gravely and earnestly by Christians who disagreed with one another. But today, these are and should be considered settled questions—even if a few people haven't quite caught up.

That is not quite true of many other issues. So many of our certainties turn out to be wrong, for we are all children of our times, limited by the perceptions of those around us. Even the points at which the church is now justifiably clear had to be worked through over a long period of time. I am embarrassed for the church when I read the words of some theologian or bishop of yesteryear defending racial segregation or opposing the ordination of women. And yet I know that the church would not be where it is today on such matters had there not been a lot of serious study and dialogue.

Similar things can be said about the troublesome personal moral decisions Christians face and which they need to address together: When should life support be ended for a patient who is a loved one? Under what circumstances should one have an abortion? What moral considerations should govern one's use of time and money, one's sexual life, one's vocational decisions? If individual Christians can immediately exclude some possible options as unworthy, it is partly because of much preceding thought and discussion within the household of faith. But now we face new dilemmas of personal morality, requiring further dialogue among Christians.

In any event, there is great need to clarify disagreements among persons of good will within the church. It is not enough simply to assume that some are right and others are wrong. All of us are right part of the time and wrong part of the time. None of us has achieved perfection in good will and commitment, but most Christians may be presumed to be at least somewhat authentic in their professions of faith. Many of the problems we confront are intellectually as well as morally challenging. We cannot bypass the intellectual puzzle by simply asserting a moral response.

Objection Four: People only speak out of their own self-interest, so serious moral dialogue is based on the illusion of objectivity. Twentieth-century "sociology of knowledge" has helped us understand a truth that oppressed people have always grasped more quickly than those who are more privileged. That is the insight that our knowledge is limited by our "social location." If we have inherited certain privileges by virtue of race, gender, economic class, and the like, we will unconsciously defend those privileges against those who do not share them. They, in turn, will speak out of *their* interest—which is to overturn the status quo. We all operate with blinders based upon our own cultural values. We tend to treat our particular interests and values as if they were universally good.

There is enough truth in this general picture to make us pause. Can any of us really *understand* the values and views of people from a different "social location"? Can white people really understand black people? Can men really understand women? Can rich people really understand poor people? Can any of us, black or white, men or women, rich or poor, think clearly about the common good? Or are abstractions like "justice" finally only expressions of somebody's self-interest? If that is so, then it might seem pointless to engage in moral dialogue. The best we could hope to do is simply to struggle for what we think to be the concrete interests of oppressed people—if we can somehow identify with them enough to make that commitment.

Actually, the limitations in our various viewpoints may be one of the best reasons for engaging in dialogue. For as we confront the view of other people, some of whom reflect very different "social locations," we have a better chance of breaking out of our own intellectual and moral limitations. Observers of the behavior of Christians in international ecumenical bodies have noted that in such settings parochial commitments and prejudices tend to broaden out. For instance, during the civil rights struggles, some southern church leaders changed noticeably when they entered into the wider dialogue in national church organizations. The same thing can occur in a local church setting provided the membership is not too homogeneous to start with.

But there is a larger theological point to be made. If we are *only* able to express the interests and prejudices of our social location, what does that imply about our ability to respond at all to God? Can God's grace be at work among us with liberating power, or are we only the creatures of some form of human self-centeredness? The church has always affirmed that people can, at least to some extent, set aside their biases and tendencies toward self-centeredness. Were that not so, the whole message of the church would seem to be pointless. Perhaps, to paraphrase a comment by Reinhold Niebuhr, we can say that there is enough limitation and bias in our individual perspectives to make a dialogue among Christians necessary, while there is enough openness and commitment to God's deeper truth to make it possible.

Is Vitality Linked to Dialogue?

In spite of these points, some may wonder whether there is any real connection between the intellectual work of the church—its thinking, its debates, its internal dialogue—and its spiritual vitality. We have all known lively churches that, if anything, appear to be anti-intellectual. The churches of the American frontier were often alive with the gospel, with vigorous revivals and intense worship. Many of the circuit-riding preachers of that day were unlettered but Spirit-filled, and the laity usually had even less education. (It is said that many Methodist preachers had to be moved every six months or so because, after that length of time, they had nothing new to say. But whether that is true or not, such preachers did shake the frontier to its foundations. Nobody could accuse them of not being faithful and spiritually alive.) Today, some of the liveliest churches are centers of a kind of vitality without being noted as centers of dialogue on the moral issues of the day. Some studies have in fact suggested that the most vigorous, growing churches in recent times have been the ones handing out the clearest absolute answers—and with no debate solicited or tolerated.

That may be true. Much depends upon what we mean by vitality, and what kind of vitality is important to us. Some kinds of liveliness are not very attractive to Christians, such as the spirit engendered at a Ku Klux Klan rally or by a political demagogue. Not all of those vigorous, growing churches with absolute answers to everything are all that appealing, either. They may not have the right answers. Indeed, one suspects that their enthusiasm is partly an escape from the pain of a confusing world, and the enthusiasm itself may be short-lived.

I am impressed by how often the great Spirit-filled

movements of Christian history expressed an intellectual wholeness as well as emotional enthusiasm. Many of the greatest Christian leaders were deep thinkers as well as lively spirits. The frontier movements of the 1800s often did have an anti-intellectual flavor. But isn't it interesting that those same movements spawned such a magnificent collection of church-related colleges and seminaries to educate the young and nurture the mind of the church?

Let us recognize that a purely intellectual approach to the gospel and to Christian moral responsibility can also be an escape—I shall have more to say about that later. But serious dialogue within the church is a part of our struggle toward wholeness. The plain truth is that we do *not* have all the answers to the important questions facing the church and individual Christians in our day. If we impose authoritative wrong answers upon those questions, we do a disservice to the gospel. We will also leave Christians with a fragmented spiritual life. To be vital in an authentically Christian sense is to be alive in all aspects of our being and to be alive to the relevance of Christian faith as it confronts all aspects of contemporary life.

The church cannot expect to have final answers on everything. But when Christians engage in serious debate and dialogue about questions that matter, they contribute to a church that matters. That was certainly true of the New Testament church. The book of Acts reports serious debates over profound issues, such as whether Gentile Christians should be compelled to fulfill Jewish initiation rites and whether the dietary laws would have to be obeyed. The church emerged stronger for the debate, not weaker. Similar things could be said about the effects of the churches' debates over civil rights and the war in Vietnam.

The failure of the church to face serious moral issues can

weaken its influence. In a study of Christian social witness during the period between the two World Wars, Paul A. Carter advances an interesting thesis about the growth of secularism during those years. It was not, he thinks, the results of godless science nor even the advance of materialism. It was, rather, that the church had only trivial answers to the important questions gripping the age. Specifically, the churches had surrendered to the crusading spirit of World War I and failed to struggle with the tragic crisis of civilization that that awful war engendered. And the churches had embraced the Prohibition movement as though it were the gospel itself, seeking legalistically to impose this upon American society. The result, according to Carter, was that most of the leading artists, writers, and philosophers—the true opinion leaders of the period—were turned off by the church.

More could obviously be said about the church during that period, including mention of some notable ways in which churches were relevant to important issues. But there is enough truth in that kind of assessment to make one wonder whether part of the lethargy of many churches today is that they have not created an environment in which people can explore ideas and problems seriously, and then do something about them. An important test of the vitality of the church is whether it can attract vital people.

But, of course, there are already vital people participating in the life of the church. As the church becomes a better community of moral discourse, we may be surprised at the effect this has in making the church "come alive."

3

Human Resources for the Church's Dialogue

A key question to be asked about any dialogue is: Who are the participants? The people who are at the table are the ones who raise most of the questions, propose most of the answers, and decide when the questions have been answered. To understand the point, consider what kind of dialogue would be likely within the church among a group of scientists, with no non-scientist present. Or among a group of lawyers, with no non-lawyers. Or among young adults. Or among millionaires. Or among homeless street people. It would be fairly limited, with issues and answers confined to a rather narrow range of concerns important to the particular group. (I *know* how limited the discussion would be if it were restricted to seminary professors!)

But if you think of all the different kinds of people who make up the church, and the even more who *could* make up the church, wouldn't a dialogue among all such people about important issues be truly exciting?

I wish, in this chapter, to suggest some of the human resources that are right at hand for the church's dialogue. I have four kinds of human resource in mind.

Those Who Are Affected Most by Problems

In some respects, the most important human resources are the people upon whom problems have the greatest impact. I am thinking especially of the people who suffer most because of the problems. The impact of racism is felt most keenly by the members of oppressed racial groups. They are the world's leading authorities on what it feels like to be oppressed in that way, and they are the ones who may be expected to insist that this problem be given attention on the church's agenda. Those who are not oppressed because of their racial identity cannot be expected to be experts in the same sense—nor are they as likely to give this problem the priority it deserves.

Similarly, poverty affects the lives of poor people more than anybody else. In the same way, they can be seen as the leading authorities on what it is like to be poor. They know first-hand the special problems they have to deal with. They are more likely to place this on the church's agenda. Other people who are not poor are more likely to be complacent about poverty. Even if they have once been poor, middle-class and wealthy people are more likely to have forgotten what life was like before; they may even congratulate themselves too much for their own accomplishment in escaping poverty. And so we can also expect women to be better experts on the peculiar burdens and oppressions culture has placed upon them—and so on with the handicapped, the elderly, youth, linguistic minorities, and those of different sexual orientation.

Such people are needed as participants when the church engages in dialogue about their special problems. Indeed, such people are needed to ensure that the church *will* engage in dialogue about those problems.

But to say that is to remember that not all of these human resources are immediately at hand. All churches probably include women as well as men, so the participation of women in discussions of women's issues may not be so difficult to come by, and most churches have at least some youth and some older adults. But many churches are in other respects relatively homogeneous. It is a rare church in which really rich and really poor people worship side by side. There are more racially integrated churches today than a generation ago, but racial homogeneity is still more the rule than the exception. Persons of homosexual orientation may be present in most churches, but they are not likely to be very visible for obvious cultural reasons.

This means that a church wishing to engage in serious moral dialogue about problems affecting persons who are not present will do what is necessary to make direct human contact. I will offer some practical suggestions about that below in chapter 6.

But it is necessary to raise the question whether this is the only kind of human resource needed. Is it enough for the victims, the sufferers, the oppressed to tell their story for the church to be able to understand what is wrong and how to deal with it? One is tempted to draw that conclusion.

Persons with Factual Expertise

The participation of those impacted by problems most is indispensable, but it is not sufficient. People almost always know *when* they are suffering, but often they do not know *why*. They may have a sense of urgency about the need for something to be done, but they may not have the best understanding of what will be most effective in dealing with the problem. A medical analogy may be helpful. When I have a headache, I know more about what it feels like than any physician does. The doctor, in order to make an accurate diagnosis, will have to ask me some questions. But he or she, by virtue of training and experience, will have a better conception than I will about the possible reasons for the headache and the most promising cures.

Similarly, poor people know the wretchedness of poverty firsthand, but they may or may not have much insight into what will contribute most to alleviating it. Some forms of special expertise, offered by people who are not poor themselves, may be helpful. Or persons of homosexual orientation know the social and cultural difficulties imposed by their sexual orientation. They may or may not have a very clear understanding of the source of their feelings and how the church and society can be most helpful to them.

So the church's moral dialogue must include the unique insights of those who are affected most by the problems of the age. But the church also needs to draw upon the knowledge of those who have special expertise. These are the people with greatest knowledge of technical aspects of problems and alternative solutions. Experts of this kind are not necessarily remote from actual human experience; rather, they have disciplined knowledge in a particular area of actual human experience. I am speaking of people who have devoted much of their lives to acquiring a particular kind of mastery.

Are such people available for the church's dialogue on moral issues? Any local church is likely to have some such people available to it, even if they are not already members. Doctors, educators, nurses, politicians, business people, labor leaders, lawyers, agriculturalists, psychologists, physical and social scientists are to be found in all cities, most medium-sized towns, and even in many smaller communities. More to the point, many of them are already members of the churches of this land. Any of the great denominations numbers among its members persons who are truly eminent authorities in all of these fields, and more. Many of them need only to be asked to participate wholeheartedly in the church's consideration of the problems it faces. One of the great tragedies of twentieth century churches is their failure to engage such experts, who are their own members.

I recall the case of one local church, in one of the southern states, whose membership included a large number of nuclear scientists employed at a major governmental installation nearby. That local church did engage these scientists in serious discussion of national policies related to nuclear energy. But, when the church offered this source of expertise to the denominational social concerns agency, it was flatly rebuffed. In doing so, I suspect the denominational leaders were trying to protect the church from being bowled over by experts who were already committed to governmental policies opposed to the church's position.

No doubt the church was right in some of its criticisms of the drift of public policy. But what the social action leaders neglected was an opportunity to make their own policy statements more informed and sophisticated. The scientists were raising questions that needed to be answered if the church did not wish to appear naive. When the church arrives at positions on issues, it needs to take into account the strongest presentation of contrary views—otherwise, its own positions will be much weaker than they need to be. That is as true in the local church as it is at the national level.

At the same time, there are some church members who

may be overly impressed by the experts. In their own judgments, the experts can be wrong as well as right. No technical experts should be considered smart enough and wise enough to settle important moral questions without further discussion.

In another context, Daniel D. McCracken has suggested that we need to take several questions into account in evaluating technical experts, such as: Is the expert really well-informed about the subject? Does the expert have a "hidden agenda," biasing his or her views? Is the expert dealing with a broad question too narrowly? Is the expert offering advice from outside his or her field of real expertise?

These are good questions, forcing us to remember that the church's moral dialogue is about more than factual issues. It is also about value questions. Highly sophisticated technical expertise can sometimes be linked to profoundly unchristian values. The net result of that can be to increase greatly the effectiveness of evil in this world!

Still, there remain large numbers of faithful Christians who are also technical experts. When they are challenged to think through the implications of their knowledge in light of their faith, the result can be exciting new insights into moral problems.

Those with Theological Expertise

Besides those who are most affected by social problems and those technical experts, the church's dialogue on moral questions needs to include those who can draw most deeply upon its central traditions. Theologians—I am using the term broadly—are the "keepers of the traditions" who are also able to make the connections between the faith of Christians and the factual world. This does not mean that theologians are themselves experts on the factual world but that they are trained to understand the theological and moral implications of facts. Moral conversation within the church needs those who know the Bible well, who have a grasp of the great streams of Christian history and tradition, who can spot the values implied by different ways of stating and resolving problems.

Does this mean that local churches must have resident theologians, biblical scholars, and ethicists present for their moral dialogues? Most of them already do. Ordained ministers are trained in seminary to be theologians, biblical scholars, and ethicists! Their role is to ask probing questions, to help others see the deeper implications of Christian faith, and to help make the connections. Of course, there are numbers of lay professionals such as Christian educators within the church who can play a similar role, along with other lay Christians who have also acquired this kind of expertise. And there are certainly many ordained ministers who are neither comfortable nor effective in this role. But the church has a right to expect it of those whom it ordains.

Do all such theologians agree on the important questions? Clearly they do not. That is a source of strength and vitality for the church, not a cause for concern. We correct one another; we supplement one another; we learn from one another. While most congregations are served by only one pastor at a time, over the years they will be served by a succession of pastors with some variations of viewpoint and emphasis. There are essentials of faith that all will share. But, pastors have a responsibility to help their congregations see a variety of different ways of stating and interpreting the faith so that the dialogue within the church will not bog down into uniformity.

Other Lay Christians

Having singled out those who are affected most by social problems, and the technical experts, and the theologians, we must ask whether other lay Christians, who do not readily fit into one of those categories, have any contributions to make as "human resources" for the dialogue.

Of course they do. Nobody should be considered "ordinary" if we mean by that a person who has no unique contribution to make. The life experience of every person is, to some extent, unique. Each of us has a wealth of experience that is not quite duplicated by that of any other person. Christians affirm that each person's encounter with God is uniquely her or his own, which means that God can be said to enter the dialogue through the mind, heart, and conscience of every participant.

Sometimes that is best expressed through the plain common sense that committed Christians can bring to bear. The body of lay Christians, taken as a whole, possesses a depth of wisdom that no single expert can claim, to the extent that the whole community of faith is willing to open itself up to the leading of God. There is some truth in the adage that "none of us is wiser than all of us." That is why many denominations do not recognize any leader as being able to articulate the mind of the church without confirmation by the church.

Many denominations provide for official church declarations by a representative body, like the United Methodist General Conference, equally made up of clergy and laity and with the possibility of on-going review. For we recognize that despite the best human resources, we still "see in a glass darkly." The church must continue, until the end of history, to seek fresh disclosures of the meaning of faith in the context of changing problems and deeper insight. And so the dialogue continues.

4

Intellectual Resources

The late Jesuit theologian John Courtney Murray once remarked that it is a "rare achievement" for people to arrive at genuine disagreement. He probably meant that we often talk past one another, not really comprehending what our supposed opponents are talking about. Sometimes we are only using different words to say the same thing. Sometimes the issues are so vague that all views and counterviews remain confused. Sometimes we are really addressing different questions, in which case the different answers may not be as much in conflict with each other as they appear to be. But it can be a real achievement for people to be so clear about their views that all parties know that there is a real disagreement.

When the church engages in dialogue on serious moral questions, its goal is consensus in the truth, not disagreement. But real consensus must be based upon clear understandings that are mutually shared, and on the way to such consensus there must be room for clear expressions of honest differences. Are there intellectual resources and disciplines that can help Christians in moral dialogue?

Beyond Intuition

A good case can be made that we arrive at our moral judgments more by intuition than by any well-defined process of thinking. That may not be all bad. Some theologians, such as Paul Lehmann, have held that true moral insight is the gift of faith more than the result of conceptual thought. "Understandably," he writes, "such an ethic will be puzzling, even ridiculous, to those who have no eyes to see the signs of the times, who do not know what belongs to their peace. Such knowledge comes by insight, not by calculation. It is the gift of faith." Most of the situation ethicists, like Joseph Fletcher, take a similar view.

That point of view does have some appeal to Christians. We all know simple but saintly folk who lack formal education and are not very articulate but who always seem to home in on what really matters. They seem to know intuitively what is at stake from the standpoint of Christian love. And, on the other hand, we all know people who can construct elaborate rationalizations for wrongdoing. In his legend of the Grand Inquisitor in *The Brothers Karamazov*, Dostoevsky develops a marvelous contrast between the elaborate rationalizations of the Inquisitor and the simple goodness of Christ. In response to the Inquisitor's lengthy justification of his demonic cruelties, Christ says nothing but simply bestows the kiss of peace. The theologians who emphasize moral character more than rational thought about morality are onto something. They are at least right in emphasizing that the instincts and intuitions of good people can generally be trusted more than the careful reasoning of bad people.

But is intuition a sufficient basis for Christian judgments about problems and issues? What happens, within the congregation, when disagreements begin to surface? Whose intuitions are to be trusted? Are we to assume that the differences of opinion really reflect underlying differences of character and spirituality? Must every disagreement, then, come down to the question of who are the real Christians with this "gift of faith" and who are not? Some of the most explosive controversies in the history of the church have been caused by exactly that attitude. Christians have been all too ready to make every disagreement a test of faith and to read those who disagreed with them out of the fellowship.

But do we have to choose between the intuitions of faith and the effort to clarify and communicate their implications intelligently? There will never be an adequate substitute for Christian love. But the task of understanding the implications of Christian love amid the complexities of this era is big enough to challenge our very best thinking. It is always possible for even the best-intentioned Christians to be wrongheaded about issues. My intentions may be perfectly loving, but my response to moral issues can have consequences that are against love. My way of dealing with one problem may be thoroughly inconsistent with my way of dealing with another one. I may blunder along and do great harm because of my failure to do my homework, to think things through carefully, and to consult with thoughtful fellow Christians. It is also true that sometimes flagrant sinners blunder, unintentionally, upon actions that (for all the wrong reasons) in fact do great good!

So how are we to go about thinking together as a church?

The Sufficiency and Insufficiency of Scripture

United Methodists recognize the centrality of Scripture. One of the official Articles of Religion speaks of the Bible as "the true rule and guide for faith and practice." In its most recently adopted statement of doctrinal standards, United Methodism speaks of the Bible as "the basic criterion by which the truth and fidelity of any interpretation of faith is measured."

One explanation of words of this kind is that the best way to conduct moral dialogue in the church is for all participants to search out the texts that speak most directly to the issues at hand. The Bible, thus, would be taken as the detailed guide for the church's moral deliberation. A contemporary movement actually calls for American law and custom to be restructured entirely on the basis of the rules laid out in Old and New Testaments. This would be something like the efforts of the Shi'ite Muslims to construct a new Iran on the basis of the Qur'an.

I suspect that few United Methodists or members of other mainline denominations are really interested in such a slavish use of Scripture. We would not want to deal with adultery or the rebelliousness of children by stoning the offenders to death. Most of us are happy that women may now speak in church, indeed that women now serve as ordained ministers and bishops. We do not think it necessarily wrong for men to wear their hair long, nor do we think women should have to have their heads covered. In addition to such points at which the cultural setting of biblical times has changed, we are more aware today of points of inconsistency in some of the specific biblical requirements. And we are all too aware that the Bible simply does not speak directly to many of our quandaries.

Still, Christian moral grounding remains thoroughly biblical. The Bible is the fundamental source of our faith. It is where we find the witness of the pioneers of that faith. All of the great themes of doctrine which serve as the bedrock of

Christian moral teaching have their roots in the Bible. So the Bible is necessary to our moral reasoning. But it is not sufficient.

That point is also recognized by the church's doctrinal statements. The Bible is the primary source and criterion, but for its essential truths to be identified and applied with clarity, Christians must also make use of tradition, experience, and reason. By *tradition* is meant the conclusions to which prior Christian generations have come as they have struggled with issues and problems. By *experience* is meant the contemporary wisdom gained by individual Christians and their churches as they seek to live out the implications of their faith. By *reason* is meant the thoughtful reflection by Christians on the meaning of faith and the attempt to appropriate all forms of human knowledge in understanding and applying the faith.

If the church's dialogue on moral questions is informed by all of this, it will be rich indeed! But the church's fourfold way of approaching theological questions (the "quadrilateral") does suggest that the discussion is likely to be complex. There is nothing wrong with that. Some issues have always been more difficult than others; sometimes we can arrive at a moral consensus rather quickly, while at other times the complexities force us to stay with it for a long time before we receive common insight.

Clarifying Our Moral Presumptions

In addressing the more complex problems, we may be helped by an approach that is familiar to all lawyers. That is the attempt to be clear about where we place the burden of proof. Legal cases are often a bit murky, with both sides stoutly defending opposite ways of interpreting the same facts. Sometimes there just aren't enough facts to justify firm conclusions. And yet, despite the confusion, the case must be decided one way or another. The law often handles such complexity by specifying, in advance, where the *presumption* should lie. Thus, for instance, it is sometimes questionable in a criminal case whether the defendant is really guilty or not. But according to law, the defendant will be *presumed* to be innocent unless it can be proved "beyond reasonable doubt" that he or she is really guilty. The burden of proving guilt has to be borne by the prosecution. What this means, practically speaking, is that if the whole case remains doubtful even at the end of the trial, the matter is decided in favor of the defendant. In civil law there are also points where the use of such presumptions is helpful. For instance, when there is (and remains) doubt about who owns a piece of property— such as land or a motor vehicle—the doubt is resolved by allowing the person who is already in possession of it to keep it. That is why those who find things are often permitted to keep them if no one else is able to establish ownership. And then, when the judgments of lower courts are appealed to higher courts, the higher court will usually presume that the lower court was right in its judgment, unless the appealing lawyers can show otherwise.

The analogy with law should not be carried too far, of course. But in dealing with difficult ethical issues we may also find it very useful to begin by clarifying our initial presumptions. In fact we probably start with such presumptions, whether or not we recognize them. For instance, in dealing with economic questions many people start with a presumption in favor of free market principles while others may look first toward government. The first group will be willing to accept a governmental solution, but only if it is proven (beyond reasonable doubt) to be necessary. The second group will accept a market-based solution, but its initial bias may be against it. Or our initial presumption may be in favor of democracy, accepting alternatives only when necessary. Or it may be in favor of peace, accepting violence only when necessary.

Much obviously depends upon such initial presumptions. In any dialogue on moral issues, especially the more complicated ones, it really would help things if people were more clear about their initial presumptions. We might find that some of those biases are not very consistent with Christian faith. We can learn that some Christians may give higher priority to one aspect of Christian faith than another, and that their disagreements with fellow-Christians come down to what seems most important. In any event, the attempt to be clear about our presumptions can help move us toward consensus—or at least toward more authentic disagreement!

It can also help us clarify what it would take to set aside those initial presumptions. Most Christians feel that war is evil, though many—probably most—are willing to accept war as a last resort. It is important, then, for such Christians to be as clear as possible about the circumstances under which they would regard war as a possible course for Christians to take. The *just war* tradition evolved through Christian history as Christian thinkers sought to clarify those circumstances. In our own time, most Christians probably consider divorce to be a very regrettable thing, yet many accept its necessity under some circumstances. The question needing clarification is, under *what* circumstances?

In these two illustrations, the initial presumptions of Christians are (1) for peace and (2) for the preservation of marriage. Reasons can be given for both presumptions on the basis of a deep reading of Christian theology. But, on the basis of that same theology, grounds can sometimes be found for exceptions.

The exciting thing about this approach to Christian moral discernment is its challenge to express the heart of the faith in morally relevant form.

Four Christian Presumptions

A book of this length cannot hope to discuss all the possibilities—if a book of any length could! But to illustrate the possibilities, four initial presumptions can be suggested. Each of these expresses fundamental Christian belief in a form lending itself to moral dialogue within the church.

The *first* is the presumption that *created existence in this world is basically good.* Such a presumption is deeply grounded in the Hebrew-Christian conception of God's creation. Despite disharmonies in nature and the evils of sickness, accidents, and death, the Christian presumption is that the world was created by God for good purposes. Taken as a presumption, this belief means that Christians will presume in favor of preserving life when either suicide or euthanasia is under consideration—though there is certainly room for discussion about extreme circumstances where euthanasia might be considered. Many Christians have had to face that awesome dilemma of "when to pull the plug." Most know, instinctively, that medical treatment should be continued as long as there is reasonable hope but that there is a time for terminating such efforts. But we may all need more preparation for such lonely decisions by thoughtful discussion of such problems with fellow Christians who can help us anticipate the circumstances under which the normal presumptions need to be set aside.

The presumption would also be that economic life is a

worthy aspect of human life and that God's loving purposes entail the meeting of human physical needs. This presumption rules out a false spiritualism in all its forms, including unnatural asceticism. One is reminded of the penetrating question of the New Testament Epistle of James: "If a brother or sister is naked and lacks daily food, and one of you says to them, 'Go in peace, keep warm and eat your fill,' and yet you do not supply their bodily needs, what is the good of that?" (James 2:15-16).

The *second* presumption is of *the value of each person's life as a child of God*. In light of God's gifts of life and grace, all persons must be presumed to possess great, even unlimited, value. On the basis of this, anything that appears to show exploitative disregard for fellow human beings must bear the burden of proof. I would also draw from this the conclusion that all human beings should receive the kind of respect that invites each to share in the social power determining the destiny of all. It also suggests that, within the limits of community resources, provision should be made for the development of each person's unique gifts and potentialities. In some communities, such a presumption would require substantial reordering of priorities.

Third is the presumption we have for the *unity of humankind in God*. Much biblical language characterizes humanity in familial or neighborly terms. We struggle to understand what this ultimately means, for our unity with one another in God is deeper than the bonds of biological or geographical or political union. We are, in a sense, a part of one another. This does not mean that we lose our individuality; Christians can understand, perhaps better than anyone, that human life is both inescapably individual and inescapably social. Our essential humanity is lost when we are treated as *only* individual or *only* as members of a community, for we are both. Taken as a moral presumption, the belief in human unity means that divisive loyalties must have the burden of proof placed against them. I see no necessary conflict here with the immediate communal values and loyalties that are important to so much of our life together. But when those values and loyalties eclipse the deeper moral reality of our oneness in God, the ancient word for that is idolatry. Much moral debate in the modern, as well as the ancient world has to do with whether we are to succumb to such idolatries. To take a very current illustration, in our discussions of national economic policy, how much weight is to be given to protecting U.S. companies from foreign competition, and for what reasons? A case can doubtless be made, here and there, now and then, for protectionist policies. But the burden of proof should be placed against proposals that treat the economic well-being of one's own country as the only relevant moral concern.

The *fourth* presumption, for the *equality of human beings*, flows more or less naturally from the first three. It is not that human beings are not unique in their gifts and possibilities; it is that no human being may be presumed to have greater value to God than any other. Social policy must, in many ways, treat different people differently, and the contributions of some are likely to be regarded more highly than others. Moreover, through the systems of rewards and punishments, which every society must have in some form or other, distinctions are made. But when distinctions imply the superiority of some people to others a very important line has been crossed. People who hold great inherited privileges are prone to consider equality a threat, but that may be what the Magnificat of Mary means by the words "he has scattered the proud in the thoughts of their hearts. He has brought down the powerful from their thrones, and lifted up the lowly" (Luke 1:51-52). A presumption in favor of equality will often have to be set aside for compelling moral reasons. But those reasons need to be clearly and carefully stated, and those who benefit most from existing inequalities must be especially on their guard lest their self-interest be substituted for Christian insight.

This last point suggests a very different kind of Christian presumption that may be needed in discussions of social issues. That is the presumption that all human beings are finite and sinful. Human beings may have been created, as the Psalmist writes, but "little lower than God" (Ps. 8:5). It seems more likely that we have been created a *lot* lower than God! And even that we spoil through the tragedy of sin. The presumption is that no person is good enough or wise enough to have total power over others. In respect to our own interests, we must reverse the usual conclusion by presuming *against* those interests when it appears that our natural inclinations have gotten the upper hand.

These are just a few suggestions. In another book on these themes, I have proposed a number of other kinds of presumptions to help guide Christian moral thought. But even that longer discussion only scratches the surface. The deeper possibilities can be opened up in the wider dialogues in which many Christians participate.

The full force of such presumptions comes from their theological roots. Superficially, such presumptions as the goodness of physical existence, or the value of individual life, or human community or equality may seem to be nothing more than humanistic abstractions that could be affirmed by anybody, Christian or not. That may be so, up to a point. But the real meaning of these presumptions derives from their source. To say that each person matters to God is a far more powerful point, with vaster moral implications, than simply to assert human value as an abstract ideal. The very fact that the presumptions can be expressed in partly secular language means, however, that they invite deeper dialogue between Christians and morally serious persons who do not yet see the point of Christianity.

5

Avoiding Pitfalls in Moral Argument

While the deeper intellectual resources Christians bring to their moral dialogues will always have theological grounding, we also need some guidance in our moral reasoning. In general, principles of moral reasoning are designed to help us say things more clearly and consistently. They spare us from saying more than we *can* say, or more than we want to say, or something different from what we thought we said. They can also spare us from saying less than we intend to say.

Principles of Logic for Moral Discourse

There are a few logical principles we do well to remember from time to time in our discussions of moral issues:

1. *General moral principles or values apply across the board to particular cases which logically fall under them.* There is a tendency in moral argument to settle things by appealing to some one general principle. Often this will be an abstraction like "freedom" or "justice." When we appeal to such a

47

principle, however, we should remember that we may not like some forms of freedom or some versions of justice. This leads to a second logical point:

2. *When a moral principle or value is appealed to in settling one moral question, it may not be disregarded when it also applies to other questions.* When I appeal to "freedom" as the reason for supporting a liberation movement in the Third World, how am I going to react when somebody else appeals to "freedom" as a reason for opposing government regulation of private enterprise? If I oppose government interventions in the economy for the sake of "freedom," can I logically oppose freedom of choice on the question of abortion? We can all readily come up with illustrations of broad general principles being applied somewhat selectively. I do not think this means we should abandon discussions based on general principles, but it does mean that we need to be a lot more careful in the way we use such principles. Rather than appealing to simple, one-word abstractions to settle arguments, we need to explain more fully what the values are that we are appealing to and what their limitations are.

When Christians appeal to "love," for instance, they need to be aware of its multiple meanings, and they need to be prepared to deal with the question whether the real interests of love require negative things to be done. And when specific sources of moral authority are cited, we must not be surprised when those same sources become an embarrassment to us in respect to other questions. I had this principle in mind when I wrote earlier that we cannot use biblical proof-texts selectively. Everybody tends to do it, but that does not make it logical. Liberals and conservatives both tend to use Bible verses when such can be found to support their case and to disregard Bible verses that are embarrassing to their views. This does not mean that we should quit using the

Bible. It does mean that the *way* we use the Bible in one context will commit us to use it the same way in other settings. I should not use a biblical proof-text to settle an argument in my favor if I do not want other biblical proof-texts to be used to settle an argument against my views on some other issue. The same thing can be said about the way we use science, or statistics, or anecdotes.

3. *We must not, therefore, misuse our sources of data and moral norms.* Sometimes we want to use whatever ammunition we can find in order to win an argument, quoting the Bible or science or statistics or anecdotes whenever they support our case and feeling free to disregard them when they do not. But this corrupts dialogue. When we use such authorities in this way it often means that our *real* reasons for taking the position are quite different from the ones we are giving out. Sometimes there is a political agenda having virtually nothing to do with the merits of the issue. We are more or less used to this in political rhetoric, where positions taken on public issues are often taken on the basis of whether particular partisan interests will be advanced or impeded— which is one reason why there is so much cynicism about public discourse in most countries. Obviously, within the church, clear moral dialogue depends upon high standards of honesty. Its purpose is to help us all to discern the truth, not to defeat our opponents.

4. *A single case is not a sufficient basis for broad generalization.* We cannot say, for instance, that all poor people are lazy just because somebody we met yesterday was both poor and lazy. Such a case may really be the exception. Much moral debate has to do with broad categories of people—racial groups, women, rich people, poor people, homosexuals, white males—as we struggle to understand the problems of justice in modern communities. We are all too prone to reach

49

premature conclusions about people on the basis of insufficient information; we stereotype whole groups of people about whom we may know very little.

5. *A single case may, however, be enough to challenge a wrong generalization.* To use the same example, if it is said that all poor people are lazy, I only have to come up with the case of one industrious poor person to show that the generalization is not well-founded. At least, those who offered such a generalization will have to change it to read that *"most"* poor people are lazy—but then we will have to ask for a lot more evidence. Fair-minded people are usually willing to acknowledge the exceptions. I happen to believe that most poor people are *not* lazy; but, in fairness, I must acknowledge that I have known some poor people who were! The very fact that a single exception is enough to destroy a generalization means that we have to make our generalizations more carefully if we expect to be taken seriously.

6. *Not all opposing values or ideas are necessarily inconsistent with each other.* Most of the foregoing logical principles are taken, more or less, from Aristotle's logic. But other philosophers, especially Hegel, have explored how apparently contradictory ideas can lead to a deeper understanding of truth that includes the truths of both sides. Much ideological debate has been wasted (and much blood spilled) in conflicts in which both sides were partly right. Earlier we spoke of the Christian insight that persons are both *individual* and *social* by nature. Some contemporary ideological debates pit these two sides against each other as though they were mutually exclusive. For instance, the libertarians are exclusively committed to individual freedom as though it were the sole principle of moral philosophy, and there are forms of Marxism and fascism that treat the social collective as the only important moral reality. But the Christian insight is that,

far from being opposed to each other, the *individual* dimension and the *social* dimension are *necessary* to each other.

In moral argument it always pays to look at the apparently opposing views to see whether there may not be a higher, more inclusive truth to which both sides are pointing. If I may draw an illustration from recent debates over feminism and the family, I am struck by the tendency of some feminists to be suspicious of family values, sometimes treating the nuclear family as little more than an expression of the long-standing cultural subordination of women. At the same time, many who are deeply committed to family-centered values consider the feminist agenda to be a prime threat to those values. But are the real concerns on both sides necessarily in conflict? Is it not true that a family in which women and men are genuinely equal is more supportive of the deepest family-centered values than a family in which men are dominant and women subordinate? And is it not true that women, as well as men, need the intimate, nurturing support of family life?

The point can also be illustrated in relation to our personal decisions. Sometimes our various responsibilities may appear to be in conflict when they really are not. Being a parent, for instance, is not necessarily in conflict with holding down a job and participating actively in community service. When people concentrate too exclusively on parenting, or their vocation, or voluntary service their lives are less likely to be whole and integrated. That may be especially evident when people do not take enough time for recreation. I have known pastors who did themselves, their families, and their churches a disservice by devoting all of their time exclusively to the work of the church. The different aspects of our lives may in fact be mutually reinforcing more than they

are in conflict, provided we keep things in proportion.

I wish to pursue this discussion, now, by highlighting several more or less typical "traps" to be avoided when we engage in moral argument within the church.

The "Straw Man" Trap

When we have strong views of our own, it is sometimes very difficult to be fair to contrary opinions. Sometimes we cut corners in argument by responding to the weakest part of those opposing opinions rather than the strongest. Sometimes, even, we will restate the opposing view in an absurd form in order to demolish it more easily. For instance, if my "opponent" doesn't like my use of the Bible, I can portray his or her position as one that does not take the Bible seriously. If he or she believes in affirmative action for racial minorities, that can be portrayed as the view that racial quotas should be adopted regardless of qualifications. A mother wishing to spend full time in parenting during the early years of her child's life can be portrayed as unliberated—just as a working mother can be portrayed as not caring about her children. A labor union seeking greater participation in company decisions can be portrayed as trying to take over. We can all think of illustrations, for the "straw man" argument is a very tempting way to win a debate.

The problem is that issues cannot be settled that way. All of us bristle at having our views and our commitments misrepresented. Nobody's views seem very compelling if we suspect that they could not face serious examination. Therefore, it is always a good discipline in our moral discussions to try to state the opposing view in its *strongest*, not its weakest, form. I'm not sure I always do this myself, but I try to teach my students in Christian ethics that they

52

should strive to state an opposing position even better than those who hold it before they go on to criticize it. If we observe this discipline we will often find that we have something to learn from others. We will certainly find that they will be more likely to learn from us if they feel we are taking them and their ideas more seriously.

"Poisoning the Wells"

This is a colorful expression used by philosophers to describe one of the typical fallacies in logic. The fallacy is to stigmatize the one who presents an idea so we don't have to deal with the idea itself. If we put poison in the well, so to speak, we will contaminate all the water that comes out of the well.

I wish this were not done as often as I think it is. It can be a real temptation to dismiss everything somebody says because they have been labeled as a liberal or a conservative, a humanist or a fundamentalist. If it has already been decided that a certain kind of people cannot possibly be right, then all we need to do is attach that label to those whose ideas we want to see rejected.

The reason this is a fallacy is that good ideas can come out of people who have been dismissed in this way. One of the tragedies of the McCarthy era in the U.S. is that the contributions of a number of very creative people were neglected after these people were smeared—most often inaccurately—as "Communist." If an idea could even be branded as "socialist" it no longer had to be taken seriously, though most people may not have had a very clear conception of what the word means nor of the contributions of socialists. Of course, the Left has also had its labels. Anyone who could be written off as a racist, a sexist, an imperialist, homophobic, or neoconservative need no longer be listened to.

The attitudes people hold do, of course, affect their ability to contribute to truth. The views of a real racist, for instance, cannot be expected to contribute to a better understanding of other racial groups. It is also true that all of us allow ourselves to be influenced by some kinds of people more than others, because we are more confident of their basic value commitments. That will be true within the life of the church, where some people generally carry more weight in discussions than others. Nevertheless, the views expressed by all people need to be taken seriously. Even if those views are entirely in error, it will serve the dialogue to examine them patiently to show *why*. We may discover along the way that most people have at least something to contribute to our greater understanding.

These observations remind us of the respect Christians pay to the humanity of even their bitterest adversaries. Our concern is not only for the truth but also for the person. Nobody is *simply* an adversary. How much more true that is of debates within the church, where we are presumably engaging one another as a part of the body of Christ. A very good discipline for any Christian congregation is for those members who have opposed one another in debate most vigorously to make personal contact immediately after the meeting is over. It helps remind us to keep the issues and disagreement in proportion. Such a reinforcing of the bonds of fellow humanity within the community of faith helps us keep from falling into the trap of "poisoning the wells" next time around.

The "Non Sequitur" Trap

The Latin term *non sequitur* is used by philosophers to speak of a certain kind of fallacy. In Latin the term literally means something that "does not follow." The fallacy occurs when we arrive at a conclusion without sufficient grounds. A crude illustration of this would be to say that everybody in this room is intelligent because they all have red hair. We may know that everybody in the room has red hair, and we may suspect that everybody is intelligent. But the fact that everyone has red hair does not prove that they are intelligent. Does this kind of fallacy ever occur in moral arguments?

Some years ago, in the midst of the Vietnam War, a prominent lay theologian made many speeches around the country in which he denounced American war policy. Fond of shocking his audiences, he used to exclaim "the Vietnam War is wrong because of the Resurrection." Without further elaboration, that is not enough. A connection could possibly be made between the theological implications of Resurrection faith and the moral value questions raised by the war. But he had not made those connections. He had simply asserted a relationship. He possibly could have argued that the Resurrection represents the triumph of suffering love, and that rather than trusting in God's love the war policy was a crude attempt to manipulate history with blunt instruments of force. But then he would have had to say more about the facts involved, and he would have had to say whether it is ever right, on the basis of the Resurrection, to act forcibly in the world. He might have noticed that others could take the view that the Vietnam War was *right* because of the Resurrection's implications concerning freedom from oppression. They, too, would have had to spell this out more carefully.

In all of our personal and corporate moral judgments we need to beware of the temptation to leap too quickly from a compelling biblical or theological insight to a conclusion that may or may not logically follow. Stewardship is an enduring

Christian moral responsibility, and that entails giving as well as wise spending. But not everything we give to—even in the life of the church—is necessarily good stewardship. Vocation is also a compelling Christian doctrine. But being "called" does not necessarily mean we are called to be missionaries or ordained clergy. Thinking together in the life of the church can be very important in helping all of us draw the right conclusions about our responsibilities.

The Law Equals Morality Trap

When outraged by blatant immoralities or social offenses, Americans are prone to say "there oughta be a law against that." In any healthy society there is bound to be a fairly close two-way connection between law and morality. The law reflects underlying moral values of the community, and moral behavior is guided by the law. Nevertheless, it is a common mistake to treat the two as though they were necessarily the same.

On the one hand, the law is not a sufficient standard for moral behavior. Many things are legal without being moral. It is, within certain limits, quite legal to speak in a cruel way to fellow human beings, but that does not come up to the moral standard of I Corinthians 13, "love is patient; love is kind." It may be legally possible to sue somebody on a pure technicality—when they are financially strapped, we are well off, and no real injury has been done. But that could also be an offense to Christian conscience. A discussion of moral issues that goes no further than the legally permissible has not yet gotten off the ground, from a Christian standpoint.

On the other hand, the fact that something does not meet the Christian standard for morality does not necessarily mean that Christians should attempt to pass laws against it.

Many people, myself among them, think it was a mistake for churches to force the absolutist position on alcohol upon the nation through Prohibition. Contemporary Christians, who wish to ban all abortions through law, should think twice whether such legislation is wise in a deeply divided community. In any event, the question whether something is moral or not is not to be treated as though it were entirely the same question as whether it should be lawful.

Premature Consensus

There is also a certain tendency to reach for agreement before all of the differences have been examined sufficiently. This is partly because we mistakenly feel that disagreement is unloving or destructive, when the really destructive thing is more likely to be suppressed disagreement that is not allowed to be expressed. There was a certain wisdom in the old Quaker tradition of waiting for the sense of the meeting. Some Quakers, no doubt, have always had more influence in the gathered meeting than others. But it was understood that no consensus really expressed the "Spirit" until it was genuinely shared by all members.

United Methodists don't go that far. We discuss things, but we also take votes. A majority can carry the day in adopting a resolution or agreeing upon a policy. Nevertheless, pushing for decision before an issue has really been worked through can be a trap that will undermine the group's integrity in dialogue.

The "Paralysis of Analysis"

The opposite danger is that of continuing to discuss questions long after most members have arrived at settled conclusions. The danger is that continued analysis may become a substitute for committed action. Most local congregations are surrounded by serious human needs to which they need to respond. Those needs should be studied and discussed thoroughly as the church reflects upon its mission. But there comes a time when it must get on with the task. I believe that a congregation must be a center for vital dialogue on important issues—as this book emphasizes throughout. But the dialogue itself is not likely to continue to be vital if it is not connected with actual mission. Perhaps the church is located in a city that has a serious drug problem. That is an important topic for sustained study and moral dialogue. But the study and dialogue will become empty if the church isn't also trying to do something about the problem. Dialogue does not have to lead to the "paralysis" trap, but we must remain alert to the danger.

The "Ritual Function"

One reason that discussion can be a substitute for action was explored helpfully by the sociologist Robert Merton. Merton's fascinating insight is that sometimes particular programs or practices serve what he called the "ritual function." By this he meant that when confronted by an unresolvable value conflict, we may deal seriously with one set of values or goals while "ritualizing" the other. For instance, a student who wants to study but who also wants to watch a football game on television may watch the game with a textbook in hand. The book won't likely get read, but a gesture has been made in that direction. If we find that solving a social problem realistically will require more time and money than we want to spend, we may use our resources elsewhere while continuing to *study* the social problem!

Politicians are sometimes adept at this. Dealing realistically with health care issues or poverty issues or criminal justice issues may require raising taxes or changing budgetary priorities which, for political reasons, the politician feels he or she must not do. But a further study or a rousing speech or even the introduction of legislation with no chance of passing can be a way of *appearing* to deal with the problems. The "ritual" has replaced a serious, realistic effort to achieve the goal.

The church, as Merton's very choice of the word "ritual" suggests, can so easily fall into such a trap! We can pray about problems, study problems, discuss problems, and take up small collections to fund totally inadequate solutions to problems, helping to create for ourselves and others the illusion that we have done something important. I do not wish to be cynical about this. Prayer, study, discussion, and offerings can be important contributions to addressing problems. Even when they are totally inadequate, they can sometimes raise the consciousness of people and lead to effective action. Still, moral dialogue within the church will be more authentic when we anticipate the ritualizing trap and avoid it.

Beyond the "Traps"

Creative moral dialogue within the church is not, of course, simply a matter of avoiding "traps" and logical fallacies. I have emphasized the pitfalls in this chapter because these are some of the points where genuine dialogue can break down.

But the whole point of this is to nurture something very positive and creative in the life of the church, to help the church come alive to its unparalleled opportunities for moral relevance in the modern world. Faced with troubling quandaries about personal moral decisions, Christians need the benefit of solid, logical thinking that is soundly rooted in the gospel. None of us is good enough or wise enough to go it alone. We need the challenge and the collective wisdom of the whole community of faith. And if that is true of our personal moral decisions, it may be all the more true of our collective responsibilities in the wider society.

In a book of this length it is not possible to outline all of the practical possibilities for structuring moral dialogue within the local congregation, even if I had the background to do so. But in the next chapter, I do wish to suggest some of the ideas that have proved useful in the congregational setting.

Questions to Guide the Church's Dialogue

Chapters 4 and 5 have dealt with intellectual resources that are available for the moral dialogue and decision-making of congregations. By way of summary, I wish to suggest several questions that Christians can ask themselves as they struggle over a difficult moral issue.

1. Do we believe that the reasons we give for our views on the issues are genuinely *Christian* reasons? Or have we allowed other kinds of values to form our judgments?

2. Do we place the burden of proof against views that, on the face of it, run contrary to what we believe as Christians? What kinds of *presumptions* actually guide our thinking?

3. What do the Bible, Christian tradition, experience, and reason contribute to the dialogue?

4. What sources of factual data are we relying upon? Are they the most dependable?

5. Are we appealing to principles and values in a consistent way, or are we using them selectively as "ammunition" to support a particular argument?

6. Have we fallen into any of the "traps" listed in chapter 5—the "straw man" trap, "poisoning the wells," the "non sequitur" trap, the law equals morality trap, premature consensus, "paralysis of analysis," and the "ritual function"?

7. Do we deal kindly and fairly with those with whom we are in disagreement, making clear that we love and respect them in spite of the disagreements?

8. Are we open to the possibility of learning from others with whom we are in initial disagreement?

6

Ideas That Have Worked

While preparing to write this book, I happened to be conducting a seminar on Christian moral decision-making with a group of local church pastors. These eight ministers, representing several different denominations and many years of local church experience, were already providing strong leadership; their congregations, so far as I could tell, were already faithful, vital centers of Christian life. The ministers were as interested as I am in making the local church a livelier place for dialogue about moral issues. What an excellent opportunity, I thought, for picking their brains about ideas and programs that really work.

A Discussion Among Pastors

I was not disappointed. One of the first comments was, "We don't need another book whipping on the pastors." I assured the group that I wholeheartedly agreed with that!

And with that point settled, the group began to compare their experiences.

One pastor, who has served different kinds of churches, also reminded us that churches are not the same. What will work in one setting may not in another. In particular, he cited the importance of how the church school is structured. Sometimes adult groups are already in place that can be encouraged to devote more attention to serious moral issues. When things are not structured that way, it may be possible to organize an ad hoc study process over a period of weeks on Sunday mornings, or weekday evenings. Sometimes, with working people, a breakfast meeting once a week for several weeks can be successful. That brought forth the remark that it can be important to conduct a study and dialogue process for a defined period of time, so that participants can have a sense of completion about it. Another pastor noted that sometimes summertime is better for experimental programs. People can be more relaxed and receptive.

One participant observed that the best discussion occurs in fairly small groups, sometimes focused upon particular age groupings. That was a good reminder that discussion of moral issues is not exclusively for adults. It can occur at almost any age level, provided the input and vocabulary are appropriate to the age.

Another pastor remarked that there is still a good deal of nervousness among churches and clergy concerning contro-versial issues in the aftermath of the conflicts of the 1960s and 1970s. He observed that it can be dangerous to deal with controversial issues exclusively in the context of the Sunday sermon where there is no opportunity for the congregation to disagree. Several of the pastors reported successful experi-ences with sermon "talk-backs." Some have structured this as a part of the service itself. One had developed a Tuesday evening program called "Second Time Around," when people could come for further discussion of moral issues discussed in the preceding Sunday's sermon. He has also experimented with involving laity in discussions of issues he plans to treat in future sermons, with further discussion after the sermon has been preached.

Several emphasized the importance of involving laity on the "ground floor" in information gathering and in structuring the process of decision-making. Authentic discussion cannot be predigested by clergy or denominational authorities. One participant reminded us of the importance of creating a climate for dialogue in which participants can make their contributions without fear of being attacked or ridiculed. An African pastor in the group spoke of the value he has discovered of involving laity in a historical perspective on how the church has failed or succeeded in addressing social issues.

Several emphasized the importance of discussion and study leading toward action. People should engage in the discussion knowing that it *will* be focused upon action. That saves the discussion from being an ivory tower exercise, and participants can have a better sense that their thoughts and words really matter.

One pastor reported on a somewhat elaborate process one of his churches had developed that aimed at getting the church to take a position on an issue as a church. The church was divided up into small clusters for meetings on a quarterly basis. Issues were posed by and for the groups, and the groups' goal was to reach consensus. The smaller groups were merged into larger ones, and eventually the whole congregation was involved. Among other things, his church developed its own mission statement through this process. The process was highly successful for three years, after which it fizzled because nobody would suggest issues any more.

Another pastor observed that that was okay. There is no problem with one or another program flourishing and then dying. When one approach no longer works, then the church must come up with another. The pastor who had used the cluster approach speculated that the real reason his more elaborate scheme eventually died was that it was too much imposed on the congregation. "It's got to come from the grass roots." Others reported instances when the impetus for dialogue originated with concerned laity.

One of the pastors also suggested the use of an outside speaker who can stir things up. It is also possible to tie in with issue-oriented television specials, such as those appearing from time to time on PBS. Sometimes program guides are available that can be sent out in advance. Another participant remarked that current audiovisuals can be excellent discussion-starters, particularly now that so many good things are available on videocassettes.

Several noted that in their experience the times of greatest congregational energy have been the times when the people have been wrestling with issues.

Our time was up, but my feeling was we had just gotten started. These eight pastors had much more to contribute, and other clergy and laity of faithful congregations across the country would be able to add to the list.

Other Ideas

I want to add a few things to the list myself, based upon many years of working with pastors and congregations seeking better understanding of their moral responsibilities as Christians.

The first point, which has already been made in various ways in this book, is that dialogue in a congregation has to be real to be very interesting to anybody. At some point, it has to be an outgrowth of real contact with actual problems. The best thing, of course, is when those who are affected most directly by a problem are actual participants—we have already seen the importance of that. That may not be as hard to arrange as one might suppose, at least in respect to local problems. If one's own congregation is a bit insulated from the effects of a problem like poverty or racism, there is likely to be some other church not too far away where those effects are felt more immediately. Why not arrange a joint task force, with people from both congregations, to explore the theological and ethical implications of the problem and the possibilities for Christian action? Such a thing must be arranged on a sensitive, non-paternalistic basis, but conversations of this kind can be conducted honestly as well.

Or, if the problem is not nearby, groups from the church can go "on location." Who would suspect a large, wealthy church in the nation's capital of developing much concern and expertise for the problems of Appalachia? Yet that is exactly what has happened in one such church as a result of youth participation in the Appalachia Service Project summer after summer. The explicit purpose of the project is to help poor people renovate their substandard housing. In fact, the youth have encountered, more or less first hand, a whole range of problems endemic to the Appalachian region—and they have wanted to talk these problems through back in their home church.

Similarly, church projects like soup kitchens, night shelters, free clinics, and clothes closets give some members of wealthier churches an immediate contact with some aspects of urban poverty problems. While such programs themselves are rarely on a large enough scale to meet the need, they can help illuminate that need and provoke serious discussion about what the political community ought to be doing. Some churches have developed significant ministries with prison inmates at the county and local level. Based on this hands-on experience, these churches are able to give serious attention to contemporary issues of crime prevention and prison reform.

At one point, *every* church has immediate access to contemporary problems: namely, the moral problems its own members face in their vocations. A whole congregation can be stimulated by examination of the moral dilemmas faced in contemporary business, or medicine, or law, or education, or public service, or agriculture. Such a discussion is especially vital to the businesspeople, doctors, lawyers, or other practitioners, but it should not be restricted to the particular group involved. The moral problems of every field are everybody's business. And all of us need the fresh insights to be gained from fellow Christians who are not personally facing the issues in quite the way we are. Why not have an annual fall or spring series of four or five weekly sessions in which the moral dilemmas of some particular vocational area are given such attention? A panel of practitioners could initiate things with their own experience, a theological facilitator could explore possible issues from a Christian perspective, some reading might be suggested. Each year, a new vocational area could be examined—with due care that the list not be restricted to the more elite professions. (Emphasizing this last point, I once served a church of over 200 members which included only three college graduates. There is absolutely no reason why that church could not engage in the same kind of moral dialogue of Christian vocational responsibility. In such discussions, everybody has *much* to learn from everybody else. And all of us need to be reminded that, to Christians, there are no elite vocations!)

Nor does this kind of format have to be limited to forms of employment. Some of the dilemmas we face are in the home, having to do with child rearing or marital problems or money management. Initial input, in a series on such things, can sometimes best be given by people with special expertise so church members will not feel they are put on the spot to reveal their own problems. But when the issues are addressed sensitively, people can be led to discuss their quandaries in the assurance that they will be understood and supported.

Periodically a similar kind of thing could be done about problems within one's city or rural county, with a focus on education, crime, welfare, banking, farming, conservation, and the like. I have in mind especially the problems being addressed by existing public and private institutions. In my experience, community leaders in all fields are eager to have an opportunity to address concerned groups of citizens, including those within the church. The church should avoid the potential trap of relying *only* on the expertise of such people, for it is above all important to probe more deeply into the meaning of the problems than most such experts have time and inclination to do. In the final analysis, the church's *theological* perspectives on such things, and the resulting motivations to do something, are its most important contribution.

Many churches have discovered that serious discussion can be prompted by a controversial action proposal or a statement or resolution on some issue that is proposed for congregational adoption. When we are put on the spot, in such a way, our minds gain a new kind of focus. I hasten to say that I do not think this should be contrived or irresponsible. It should be a serious proposal, based upon Christian motivation and an appropriate sense of urgency. But such proposals can then bring extraordinary vitality to the church's dialogue.

I shall never forget what proved to be one of the great moments of dialogue in the community life of my theological seminary. In 1984, when groups of protesters were picketing the South African embassy in Washington, D.C., the seminary community was asked to take responsibility for the picketing on a designated day two or three weeks ahead. At the time, such picketing in front of an embassy was illegal (that law was itself subsequently found unconstitutional by the courts), so the seminary students, faculty, and staff were being invited to participate in an act of civil disobedience with the probability of being arrested. Most of us took the invitation seriously, for we shared the conviction that South African apartheid is a monstrous evil and that the embassy demonstrations could be effective as a way of arousing greater public awareness.

The prospect of picketing the embassy at least increased awareness within the seminary community! There was more serious discussion of Christian ethics within that two- or three-week period than any other whole semester. None of us could escape the question, would *we* participate? So we were all driven to the most searching examination of the issues and of the theological foundations upon which we should decide. In the end, many participated and did so with an assurance that would never have been possible without the opportunity for dialogue with fellow Christians.

When the proposal was made for a new constitutional amendment guaranteeing citizens of the District of Columbia voting representation in both the U.S. House and Senate, members of one United Methodist church proposed that the church adopt a resolution supporting the amendment and recommending that it be supported by the church's General Conference. The idea was controversial, and a whole discussion process developed within the church, touching upon very fundamental issues of theology and political philosophy. In the end, the resolution was adopted and, subsequently, the General Conference did concur in supporting the amendment. Whether such a proposal is or is not adopted can depend upon the merits of the case and the quality of the discussion. Obviously the quality of the discussion and the health of the church depend upon the church's observance of the kinds of disciplines suggested in previous chapters, especially those having to do with respect for the personhood and views of those with whom we are in disagreement.

We need not fear disagreement. The social action committee of a church with which I was associated in the early 1970s struggled with the question whether it should hold an evening program on the Vietnam War. Within that church, as well as in the nation at large, the war was very controversial—so much so that people were afraid of disrupting the church. It was finally decided to hold such a program, with one speaker from the U.S. State Department defending U.S. policy and another speaker from a peace organization criticizing it. In deference to the fears, it was decided that only written questions would be entertained from the floor so that nobody could grab a microphone and disrupt things. That measure proved completely unnecessary. Both speakers were civil, showing obvious respect for each other's views, and the questions were phrased thoughtfully and carefully by most of the audience. It was clear, in the end, that the church was a good deal healthier for having brought the issue out into the open in this way than it would have been if disagreement had continued to simmer under the surface.

Should a local congregation explore overtly political issues? Since most issues have a political dimension, we can hardly avoid doing so if we intend to deal with the real world in our moral deliberations. Some may feel, nevertheless, that it is a mistake to address particular electoral campaigns within the church.

There are indeed some real risks in appearing to put the church on record in support of one candidate or party against another. I respect the churches, especially within minority communities, that are willing to run those risks for what they consider to be compelling reasons—though in the main I think it is best not to do so. Short of that, a local congregation can do a lot to foster serious ethical consideration of the issues and candidacies that develop during a campaign. One rural church of my acquaintance used to sponsor a series of candidates' nights, with one night for each office up to and including the congressional race. Candidates were invited to come and make a presentation and then submit to questions from the audience. But the invitation specified some of the issues the church expected the candidates to address, and when the issues were ducked that was embarrassingly evident to everybody. No effort was made to arrive at a "sense of the meeting," but everybody—including the candidates—was stimulated to think more seriously about important public issues. Incidentally, most candidates— even at the congressional level—were quite eager to accept the invitation.

Another church, in an urban setting, developed a series of four Sunday morning forums during a presidential election campaign. This was structured with one major issue being considered each week. The same two speakers made presentations each week on these issues, with one articulating the Republican view and the other the Democratic view. The speakers alternated weeks in their assigned party positions. Only on the last week did they indicate which way they planned to vote, and why. Such a discussion series does not commit the church to one side or the other, but it can stimulate informed debate within and beyond the church on the basis of deeper ethical and theological considerations.

This chapter has presented a number of concrete suggestions, but I return to the observation of one of the pastors in my seminar: every church is unique, and what will work best in one setting may not in another. Churches should experiment with ventures in moral dialogue and not be disappointed if some ideas are not as good as others for them. I am confident that *every* church can do some very interesting things—and that *any* church will be livelier and more faithful to the gospel if it engages in serious moral dialogue about issues that matter.

But how does this relate to other aspects of the life of the congregation? We turn next to that question.

7

Connections Within the Congregation

There is a certain vague suspicion among many Christians that controversial issues diminish the vitality of the congregation. Some would say that preoccupation with social issues is one of the big reasons for the declining membership of mainline denominations in recent years. People pack up and leave when views are proclaimed that they believe to be wrong, or even when the climate of church life is too heavily burdened by conflict and stress.

Obviously I do not agree with that basic assumption. I believe that a healthy dialogue on moral issues, even controversial ones, is a key to congregational vitality, not a source of weakness. But it can make a real difference *how* issues are raised and whether this dialogue is well-connected with other aspects of the life of the church.

In this chapter I wish to discuss some of those connections.

Preaching and Worship

When many people think of controversial issues in the church, they may instinctively associate them with preaching, for it is through preaching that ideas and applications are dealt with most visibly in most churches. The sermon is, in fact, a quite remarkable invention. It is most associated with Christian worship, indeed with Protestant Christian worship. It is an awesome opportunity for any preacher to be able to mount the pulpit week by week and proclaim the faith, as he or she understands it, before a fairly receptive, usually complaisant audience of people who believe it would be impolite to disagree. What a golden opportunity to place serious issues on the agenda for thoughtful discussion in the life of the church. The opportunity is sometimes abused. It is abused if the implication is ever left that only the preacher has an opinion worth hearing. The preacher is indeed likely to have special credentials for exploring the theological and moral ramifications of issues—for it is her or his professional responsibility to be well-grounded in the Bible and other Christian sources and to be a disciplined theological thinker. But, as we have already made clear, everybody else in the life of the church has important contributions to make as well. The ministers referred to in the last chapter, who have experimented with sermon talk-back sessions and seminars, have recognized that theirs is a shared responsibility.

Preaching about serious moral issues can also be a problem when preachers do not do their homework. I still remember a curious phone call I received some years ago from a United Methodist minister in a neighboring city. He had preached a controversial sermon the day before and had stirred up a hornet's nest of reaction. He was calling to be sure he had been right in his facts about the issue. After hearing him out, I assured him that in my opinion he was, in fact, on the right track. But I also had to remind him that the time to do one's research is *before* preaching a sermon, and not *after*!

This much acknowledged, I want to raise a more serious question for those who still feel that sermons should avoid controversy. What does it do to the integrity of a worshipping community if the people feel, deep down, that the preacher is only going to say what they want her or him to say? Granted preachers can be wrong. Granted, also, that the whole congregation needs to get into the act, with everybody making their contributions. Granted, further, that everybody should do their homework. What is the deep effect on the spiritual life of people if they know that what is said will only be a projection of what they already are? Can they have any confidence that God will be able to speak to them in fresh ways in the worship setting? When we muffle the application of the Word to current issues, are we unwittingly stifling the voice of God?

Preaching is, of course, but one part of the worship life of the church. It is arguably the most important aspect for the consideration of moral questions, but other aspects are also very important. Even so commonplace a thing as our choice of hymns can contribute or detract from moral sensitivity. Many Christians take the words more or less for granted, and wide latitude is granted for excesses of poetic license. Nevertheless, the lyrics of the hymns we sing reinforce deep attitudes that are quite relevant to the issues we face.

That is also true of prayer. What do we express thanks for in our prayers? That can be very revealing of our deeper values! Are we too grateful for our material blessings, not grateful enough for the greater gifts of love and opportunities to serve? Are we grateful that we have been spared some awful catastrophe that has wreaked devastation in the lives of others, thus separating ourselves from those sisters and brothers and questioning the evenhandedness of God's love? Or in our prayers of confession, what do we consider the sins to be that are serious enough to warrant confession? Do we speak of fairly minor things, avoiding consideration of the monstrous evils—in which we may indirectly participate—that lay waste to God's loving intentions for humankind on earth? Or, as we pray for others, do we do so in a way that conveys self-righteousness and division or in a way that acknowledges the need for healing the brokenness of community? Are our petitions for guidance and for forgiveness informed by the church's on-going dialogue about moral issues?

The connections between the worship life of a church and its moral dialogue and action are very deep. Worship, as the word itself suggests, is at the center of our valuing. We worship what has *worth*. God is the source of all worth. In worshipping God, we are drawn into the perspective of God on all things, and we come to value things more as God values them. There is, therefore, a two-way street between congregational worship and congregational dialogue. Worship draws us to the sources of wholeness and drives us to bring our lives and our world into this wholeness. Dialogue raises questions that we must bring before God.

The church's study and dialogue are therefore important in keeping our worship honest. Sermons, prayers, readings, other materials, should not presuppose answers to questions that, in all honesty, still need to be kept open. In worship we may not assume that people agree with a factual analysis that has not yet been made clear. Sometimes it is better and more honest to point to an area of concern, acknowledging our confusion and our need for more faithful study and action.

Pastoral Care

It is also sometimes thought that consideration of controversial issues is the opposite of pastoral care. Some people still appear to believe that there should be a kind of division of labor between good pastors—who attend to the spiritual and emotional lives and problems of the flock—and the social prophets, who stir things up with their controversial sermons. Such a division of labor does violence to the wholeness of faith to which we are *all* called. Was the word of Jesus to the rich young ruler only prophetic and not also pastoral? Or only pastoral and not also prophetic?

What, after all, does *pastoral* mean? Surely, within the church, it is not a synonym for private therapy modeled after psychiatric practice. Its great meaning, in Christian tradition, is the "cure of souls," which in turn refers to our wholeness in the faith. Anything that disrupts that wholeness, reducing our lives to fragments, is a pastoral problem. Death can be a serious pastoral problem, not only because of the rupturing of close relationships that are precious to us, but because it so often poses a crisis of trust in God. Seen in this perspective, is it not also a deep pastoral problem that in our actual existence, in this broken world, we are forced to live as though the Kingdom of God were unreal? How can desperately poor or racially oppressed people believe in God's love while their suffering is allowed to continue, with no end in sight other than the abyss of death? Many find it possible to trust in a God who, after death, can raise their lives to a new level of blessedness; but even so, the powerlessness of God to confront the evils of this world in their behalf has been conceded. On the other hand, how can those of us who do not suffer from such oppression be whole in the faith as long as we live in a world filled with people who do? Does it not raise even for us the question of the powerlessness of God? It is remarkable that many Christians are still able to discern the power of God's grace at work in the world, in spite of all the contradictions. But it is no wonder that those contradictions overwhelm the consciousness of large numbers of people.

The need for social reform remains at the center of authentic pastoral care. For a church to be struggling with the problems of actual existence is for the church to be pastoral in the best sense. (Recent pronouncements by the Roman Catholic Church—such as the "Pastoral Constitution for the Church in the Modern World" of the Vatican Council—help to recover this broader understanding of the word *pastoral.*)

But even in the best of all possible worlds, which this will not be until the end of history, there will be pastoral problems beyond the cure of social reform. We can still find ourselves torn apart by moral guilt over personal and professional transgressions and in need of restoration to wholeness. Personal therapy may, even in that best of worlds, have a role to play. But repentance and redirection, grounded in the faith of the church, can be more basic.

One more point should be made about this. The personal and the social are united in the spiritual life of Christians. The greatest Christian prophets have often been people who were deeply grounded in their own spiritual lives. In season and out, year by year, such people are able to face the frustration of important causes without abandoning their commitments.

Evangelism

If pastoral care, traditionally speaking, is "soul curing," evangelism is understood as "soul winning." What does *that* have to do with the church being a community of moral discourse?

More than most people think. To be persuaded of the gospel and to surrender oneself to God as revealed in Jesus Christ, one must first have some understanding of what that *means*. Does it mean that one accepts God's saving grace, with no implications whatsoever for one's relationships and the way one lives? Some Christians have appeared to believe that, but that implies that Christian morality does not matter and that God has no concern about the created world—both of which are startling heresies! Does it mean that Christians commit themselves to act lovingly in the immediate setting and to be concerned about relationships with those whom they know directly—but not to care much about people they have never met or about large scale patterns of relationship that extend beyond the immediate environment? Is God so small? Is Christian responsibility so limited?

Real evangelism interprets the whole world in light of God's saving grace and invites people to identify themselves with that understanding. Like pastoral care, evangelism seeks to overcome the broken, fragmented life of this world with a wholeness grounded in God's love and creative purposes. Such evangelism is not limited to a list of proven techniques or a purely individualistic appeal. It is, in its own way, an attempt to transform a whole culture with ever-new values based on the gospel.

For example: When a society defines some people as inferior because of the color of their skin or the menial but useful work they perform, that is bad news for those who are defined as inferior. But it is also bad news for everybody else, because the implication is that what matters about life is the color of our skin or the prestige of the work we do. The good news is that human value is deeper than that; specifically that

God loves us regardless of such things. An implication of this, which is also good news, is that there are valuable contributions that everyone can make to the life of the community.

Another example: When the culture glorifies violence that is bad news for all of us, because it means that human beings are really in a hostile environment where it is each one for him- or herself. The good news is that we belong to one another in God and we can work, along with God, in overcoming the tragedy of violence in this world.

When the Christian community struggles together to understand cultural issues of this kind in light of Christian faith, it is engaged in important preparation for the work of evangelism. When it engages in evangelism, it draws upon much previous thought and discussion about the meaning of Christian faith in the circumstances of contemporary life.

Mission

The word mission, like evangelism, sometimes conjures up images of individualistic efforts to save persons from the clutches of competing religions—usually in other countries. Such a truncated understanding of mission is remote from the thinking of most United Methodists today. The word is seen in broader terms referring to the church's task to witness to the gospel and act out its implications throughout the world.

Must we choose between acts of service and communicating the meaning of the gospel? Must we choose between direct hands-on ministries to persons in need and advocacy for such persons in the corridors of power? Surely these are false choices. The church must be at work in service *and* witness, in advocacy *and* direct immediate action. All of these dimensions are strengthened when they are seen in a broader missional context with the others. It strengthens our ministry to persons in need when we can, with integrity, announce that we are doing this because we perceive them, in God, to be our sisters and brothers. Often, as a matter of fact, the deepest need that people have is to see their own lives as valuable. Similarly, our hands-on ministries, the soup kitchens, the clothes closets, the night shelters and health clinics, provide the kind of direct information about social forces and social needs that give us an incontestable basis for advocacy.

All of this is undergirded by study and dialogue within the church.

I have a confession to make to United Methodist women. During my seminary student days I questioned the value of the small study books used, trivially I thought, in the various women's groups throughout the land. Then, as a graduate student, I wrote a doctoral dissertation about the racial struggle within the church. I discovered, to my surprise and delight, that the women were leading the whole church. Why? It was partly *because they had learned so much while reading and discussing those study books!* The books, it turns out, were pretty good. The discussion brought their message into the local context and helped inspire and direct large numbers of women to be real actors in the struggle to liberate the church and society from the demons of racial segregation. I do not want to overstate the point. But it is clear to me now that that kind of study and discussion really does matter.

This chapter has attempted to show connections between Christian moral dialogue within the church and some of the standard, well-accepted aspects of the life of the local congregation. Let us summarize the implications of this chapter with a blunt question: Is it really possible for the church to have authentic worship, to practice evangelism, to be pastoral, and to claim its larger mission without also being a community of moral discourse and dialogue? I do not think so.

8

The Local Church and the Universal Church

The focus of this book has been the local congregation as the community of moral discourse. I make no apology for that: the church will probably be no stronger and no weaker than its local congregations. That is where the Christian life of most of us is centered; that is where we worship, where we are nurtured, where we are challenged to be about our vocations as Christians in the world.

But United Methodism is also a connectional church, with well-forged links between local, regional, national, and worldwide levels. United Methodism is, moreover, deeply committed to the ecumenical church, recognizing its interconnectedness with councils of churches at different levels and engaging in dialogues and common ventures with other denominations across the nation and world. So, when United Methodists speak of *church* they refer not only to the local congregation but also to the wider expressions of the church universal. What are the implications of this for the church's moral dialogue?

A Two-way Street

Such a dialogue occurs at all levels, and both denominationally and ecumenically. It is a mistake to take only one of the settings as being where the "real" debate is taking place, while disregarding the others. The United Methodist *Book of Discipline* makes clear that only the General Conference speaks for the church as a whole. But it would be a mistake to conclude from this that only the General Conference can speak. *Everybody* can and should speak—and listen. The positions taken by a General Conference and embodied in the *Discipline* or the *Book of Resolutions* are a resource of great value to the local congregation. At the general church level it is often possible to draw material and intellectual resources together that are not available to local congregations. The resulting work is often more sophisticated, and it is usually worthy of serious consideration by local congregations. On the other hand, what happens at the local grass-roots level constantly feeds and occasionally challenges the broader levels. I wish to say more about how this two-way street functions.

The Local Church's Contribution

One of my pleasant surprises, as a delegate to the 1988 General Conference, was to discover just how seriously that body was impacted by local congregations. I already knew that every local church (or any individual United Methodist, for that matter) is entitled to send petitions to the General Conference and actually have them read by somebody. What I had not realized is the extent to which the petitioning process structured the actual agenda of the Conference nor how many local churches took it upon themselves to present their views in letters to delegates. In the flood of letters from local congregations, the sameness of some of the letters suggested that the basic thinking had been done for these churches by caucuses of one kind or another. (There is nothing wrong with that, but it is not necessarily a grass-roots expression of considered opinion.) But many of the letters and resolutions obviously reflected careful consideration by this or that local congregation. Some of these statements dealt with previously unconsidered problems and shed new light on old issues. At the very least, such letters conveyed a direct sense of the rich diversity of the whole denomination. Often they made substantive intellectual contributions.

The commitment by the General Conference to receive and process all such communications makes one wonder what would happen if every local congregation were to take advantage of this opportunity to make its views known. I'm sure a way could be found. But I am also sure that focusing on issues for a General Conference is a very good way for a local congregation to initiate and carry out moral dialogue.

I referred earlier to a southern congregation in which a number of nuclear scientists sought to influence the general church with their views. It is a pity they were not invited into the denominational debate at the time. But there is a sequel to the story. Later, after the United Methodist bishops had published their pastoral letter, *In Defense of Creation*, a dialogue was set up between members of this local church and a number of the bishops who were meeting in a nearby city. The discussion did not lead to total consensus, but the bishops and the local church participants reported that it had been a growing experience on both sides. The church's pastor reported that a prominent physicist who participated in the dialogue remarked that "Before this weekend, it never occurred to me that there is a connection between what I do in the lab and who I am as a member of the church."

It is usually easier for a local church to have visible impact on the positions taken by a regional judicatory, like an Annual Conference. Such bodies do adopt resolutions and carry out programs, and these statements and programs are likely to be better thought out if local churches have participated conscientiously in the process. Focusing on this level has the added advantage that local churches have clergy and lay representatives in Annual Conferences who can make the case directly and bring first-hand reports back after the Conference is over. People in local churches sometimes complain that everything in the church comes down from above. That has never been quite true; but the key to making this a two-way street is in the local church itself. All of the legal procedures are in place granting churches full access to regional and denominational bodies and, with some qualification, to ecumenical bodies as well.

The Connectional Contribution

Regional, denominational, and ecumenical bodies also have important contributions to make to the moral dialogue within local churches. I have three things in mind.

First, the connectional and ecumenical church can, in various ways, help free the church from the effects of local biases and intellectual blind spots. The more universal levels of church life are likely to be more inclusive. At those levels, participants rub shoulders with persons they have never encountered locally who must now be taken more seriously. Also, at those levels participants are challenged to do their thinking more explicitly as Christians and not be quite as influenced by secular interests and values.

Statements and actions by the denomination or by the National and World Councils of Churches are not above criticism, of course. But some of the more irresponsible criticism has come from people who reveal, thereby, their own lack of perspective. A local setting can be insulated from important realities and viewpoints needing to be heard. Even a denomination needs the correction of perspectives from other confessional traditions. At the world level, no one national group can dominate, and the result is likely to be a more authentic witness to the God of all nations.

A second contribution to the local church is to provide resources for the discussion of moral issues that are more sophisticated than could be developed locally. I do not think such resources can ever be an adequate *substitute* for serious discussion within a local congregation; they should not be accepted unthinkingly simply because they have been handed down by distant authorities. But they can make an enormous contribution to the quality of local church discussion.

The United Methodist *Book of Resolutions* is one illustration of such resources. This book is a voluminous collection (608 pages in the 1988 edition) of statements and resolutions adopted by the General Conference. The current edition contains the Social Principles document of the denomination and thoughtful statements on such issues as the crisis of rural communities, U. S. energy policy, suicide, abortion, war and peace issues, economic policy, drug and alcohol concerns, affirmative action, Native American affairs, health care delivery, genetic science, and capital punishment. There are about 187 statements in all. Arguably that is too many for the church to address with high quality, and some of the declarations clearly are better than others in articulating the relationship between Christian faith and the issues of the day. (I could point out a few of the statements that are contradictory or based on sloppy or one-sided research.) But many of the statements do reflect great care in preparation. Sometimes they originate with agencies of the church, such as the General Board of Church and Society; sometimes they are proposed by annual conferences, or even by local churches. Often they include substantial research and the involvement of persons with special expertise. Reasonable people can be helped to think through issues with the aid of this kind of resource, whether or not they wind up agreeing with the general church's position. I suspect that not many local churches take the trouble to discuss these resolutions seriously, but they could and the denomination's own positions could be improved next time around as a result.

In recent years the United Methodist Council of Bishops, utilizing a pattern also developed by the Roman Catholic Bishops, has provided such leadership through the publication of lengthy pastoral letters. Such documents, while they have no official standing as declarations of The United Methodist Church (unlike the Roman Catholics), can be an excellent way to raise issues and help people see faith connections. The 1986 Pastoral, *In Defense of Creation*, was an especially good illustration. The letter, together with its supporting background document, comprised a book-length analysis of the theological and moral implications of preparations for nuclear war. It proved to be controversial; but even many of those who disagreed with parts of it found this to be a very helpful contribution to moral dialogue on the life-and-death issues it discussed. The value of the letter was greatly enhanced by much advance consultation with authorities of diverse viewpoint and by a dialogue process at the local level.

The U.S. Catholic bishops' widely acclaimed 1986 Pastoral

Letter, *Economic Justice for All*, was another good illustration of this process of involving a wide range of experts and Christians at the local level. The quality of the document helped account for the extensive coverage it received in national media, making it uniquely accessible to thousands of local churches throughout the land.

Annual conference resolutions, much maligned as they are, can reflect a broader range of expertise. Sometimes they are poorly prepared and adopted in a perfunctory way, which is a pity because the factual and theological resources available to annual conferences are considerable. The point was demonstrated pointedly at the 1989 session of the Baltimore Annual Conference. A resolution had been put together in some haste in an effort to put the Conference on record about the Tiananmen Square repression in China. Some dissatisfaction was expressed with the strident tone of the declaration, and with its uncertain factual grounding. Two lay members of the Conference then identified themselves as career diplomats with the State Department and offered their experience and expertise in making the statement more reasonable and effective. Not many Annual Conferences are likely to have career diplomats as lay members (and even those that do should not accept their contributions without critical examination). But my point is that all Conferences have a broader range of human resources available to them than does any local congregation.

A special word should be offered about the National and World Councils of Churches. These bodies have drawn the attention of demagogues as well as more responsible critics, but the depth and thoroughness of some of the ecumenical documents is not well known at the local church level. The series of Assemblies of the World Council of Churches, commencing with the Amsterdam Conference in 1948, has produced some of the best commentary on twentieth-century moral dilemmas available anywhere. These Assemblies, and the preparatory process leading up to them, generally engage the thinking of leading theologians and secular experts in a variety of fields. Christian thinking about the conflict between Communism and Capitalism was greatly advanced by the extraordinary analysis given at Amsterdam and the previous Oxford Conference of 1937. A special section of the Evanston Assembly of 1954 on race relations tapped the expertise of the American Benjamin Mays and the South African Alan Paton. Well-known world intellectual leaders, ranging from the anthropologist Margaret Mead to the economist Denys Munby, have made similar contributions.

I do not wish to issue a blanket endorsement of everything produced by such bodies. But local churches impoverish themselves when they do not take advantage of such resources.

Third, the connectional church provides opportunities for broader personal contact and service. This does not have to be limited to a handful of church representatives and leaders. From time to time, at the regional and national levels, events are held to which people are invited from all churches. Even were that not the case, the fact that The United Methodist Church includes very diverse local congregations means that any congregation can locate sister congregations to help overcome the insulations to which we may all be prone.

If all moral dialogue is finally aimed toward service, it must not be forgotten that at the denominational and ecumenical levels the relative weakness of individuals and small congregations is overcome in the merged strength of all. Denominational and interdenominational programs are not substitutes for local action, but they can accomplish things that are beyond the resources of any one group.

Conclusion

Everything we do in the church is affected, for good or ill, by the quality of our thinking together. I have sought to make the point in various ways that the local church can become a vibrant center for moral discourse and that this will make that church overall more alive. In this chapter I have made the concluding point that the vitality of the church universal also depends on how this is done locally, just as the local church can be greatly enlivened by the contributions at the broader levels.

Sources and Suggested Further Reading

References to the history of United Methodist discussion of social issues in chapter 1 are informed especially by Richard Cameron, *Methodism and Society in Historical Perspective* (Nashville: Abingdon Press, 1961) and Walter G. Muelder, *Methodism and Society in the Twentieth Century* (Nashville: Abingdon Press, 1961).

Walter Rauschenbusch's devotional classic, referred to in chapter 2, is his *For God and the People: Prayers of the Social Awakening* (Boston: Pilgrim Press, 1910). His comment on the unchristian social order is from *Christianizing the Social Order* (New York: Macmillan, 1912). Sources for the second objection in chapter 2 include John Howard Yoder, *The Politics of Jesus* (Grand Rapids: Eerdmans, 1972) and Stanley Hauerwas, *A Community of Character: Toward a Constructive Christian Social Ethic* (Notre Dame and London: University of Notre Dame Press, 1981). Paul A. Carter's view is contained in his book, *The Decline and Revival of the Social Gospel* (Ithaca, N.Y.: Cornell University Press, 1956).

The Daniel McCracken questions in chapter 3 are from his

thesis, "Ethical Problems of the Expert Witness in National Decision Making Involving the Assessment of Technology" (unpublished B.D. thesis, New York: Union Theological Seminary, 1970), pp. 42-50.

The Paul Lehmann quotation in chapter 4 is from his *Ethics in a Christian Context* (New York: Harper and Brothers, 1963), p. 141. More extended discussion of the use of Christian moral presumptions is contained in J. Philip Wogaman, *Christian Moral Judgment* (Louisville: Westminster/John Knox Press, 1989).

Robert Merton's description of the "Ritual Function" in chapter 5 is from his *Social Theory and Social Structure* (Chicago: Free Press of Glencoe, 1957).

The United Methodist Bishops' Pastoral, referred to in chapter 8, is *In Defense of Creation: The Nuclear Crisis and a Just Peace* (Nashville: Graded Press, 1986). The Roman Catholic Bishops' Pastoral is *Economic Justice for All: Pastoral Letter on Catholic Social Teaching and the U. S. Economy* (Washington, D. C.: National Conference of Catholic Bishops, 1986).